WARSHIPS in COLOUR

Copyright Irwell Press,
ISBN-978-1-906919-41-2
First published in 2011 by Irwell Press Ltd., 59A, High Street, Clophill, Bedfordshire, MK45 4BE
Printed by Konway Press.

The Warships were amongst the most controversial of the early BR diesel classes; the WR management had to fight tooth and nail to get them built in the first place and they were continually attacked by the diesel-electric proponents until they were taken out of service prematurely in the early 1970s under the guise of standardisation.

They carried the standard BR green livery with a grey horizontal lining band, enhanced from 1962 by the addition of small yellow warning panels on the nose-end. Almost half were repainted during1965/6 in the maroon which had been adopted for their Western contemporaries, before the majority were given BR's Corporate blue livery which it has to be said did nothing to improve their appearance, even though it was not dissimilar to the colour originally recommended but subsequently rejected in 1959. The Warships became Class 42/43 under TOPS but new numbers were not applied because they were pencilled in for early withdrawal under the National Traction Plan.

There were only a few noticeable changes over the fourteen years the locomotives were in service. Those built without train indicator panels had them added, the multiple working equipment was taken off and restored, and there were minor changes on the nose-ends of some locomotives.

The Warships were originally employed primarily on the Western Region Paddington-Bristol and West of England services, venturing onto the North-West line up to Crewe between 1962 and 1964. They took over the former SR Waterloo-Exeter trains in 1964 where they held sway until October 1971. In 1967 the North British built locomotives were tried on the Paddington-Birmingham passenger services but after numerous failures they were quickly removed from this work, although they did take over the Worcester/Hereford services which they worked until 1971. The class was ousted from much of their principal WR express work in the mid-1960s, but they did stage a brief comeback in 1968 when pairs of Warships were employed on the accelerated services to the West of England. Over their last few years they were to be found increasingly on freight and secondary workings before the final survivors succumbed in late-1972.

Two D800s escaped the cutters torch and although neither has been on the mainline they have both appeared at many preserved railways and open days over the years.

Acknowledgements

I would not have been able to produce this volume without the assistance from a number of photographers and I would like to record my thanks especially to Michael Mensing, Hugh Ramsey, Terry Berry, and Rail-Online for the use of their superb pictures, and to Martin Street who has trawled through the captions, correcting my errors and adding much additional information in the process.
John Jennison, 2011.

D600 ACTIVE at Old Oak Common on 12 November 1961 alongside D803 ALBION. The D600s would only be found in the Capital for another six months or so, after which they were restricted to working west of Newton Abbott. ACTIVE has gained the train reporting number frame and vertical louvres since it was introduced in January 1958. It received full BR Corporate blue in April 1967, only months before the whole class was withdrawn at the end of that year. (www.rail-online.co.uk)

D601 ARK ROYAL in 1960 on the 'Cornish Riviera Express' in chocolate and cream garb passing through a deserted Holt Junction. It must have been diverted from its usual route between Westbury and Woodbrough via Lavington. D601 is in original condition, still with horizontal louvres although the brackets to hold the train headboard have been removed and it is now suspended from the upper lamp holder. ARK ROYAL, which retained its green livery until the end, was the last survivor of the class, remaining at Woodham's scrapyard in Barry, South Wales for more than a decade after withdrawal in 1967 and was not cut-up until June 1980. (CTLS)

D602 BULLDOG at Swindon on 17 June 1962 where it had been fitted with a replacement transmission from Type 2 D6302 during a Heavy Casual overhaul, and was recorded as off-works three days after this picture was taken. It received its yellow warning panel on its previous works visit between February and April. (Hugh Ramsey)

D602 BULLDOG at Laira in July 1968 with D603 CONQUEST behind, over six months after their withdrawal at the end of 1967. BULLDOG received an early version of the new BR blue livery with a flat-topped small warning panel in December 1966, the train indicator boxes having been fitted in late-1964. The numbers are the old serif style and the centrally positioned double arrow is the small version. The two locomotives were towed away together with D604 by D1006 on 29 July to Cashmores at Newport and were cut up by the end of November.

D800 SIR BRIAN ROBERTSON on 16 May 1959 between Truro and Chacewater nears the end of its journey with the down 'Cornish Riviera Express'. The immaculate chocolate and cream Mark 1s suited the GWR-style green of the Warships. D800 would return later from Penzance with the 7pm to Paddington. (Michael Mensing)

D800 SIR BRIAN ROBERTSON at Bristol Temple Meads on the westbound 10.10 Bradford-Paignton 'Devonian' on 1 August 1968, a few weeks before it was taken out of service. The only member of the class with a single line name without the 'Warship Class' below, it was fitted with standard route indicator box and longer horizontal grab rails in March 1964.

An immaculate D801 VANGUARD at Basingstoke on 10 May 1967 with the 13.00 Waterloo-Exeter. It was the first of the Swindon designed Warships to be withdrawn, in August 1968 still wearing the maroon livery which it had received in June 1966. (www.rail-online.co.uk)

D802 FORMIDABLE was the only one of the first three D800s to carry green, maroon and blue liveries. Its final repainting, just a year before withdrawal, was in October 1967 when it was called into works for an external repaint into blue. In this photograph at Bristol it has the early double arrows positioned on the cabsides underneath the serif numbers. In early 1964 the frame for the reporting numbers was replaced by the standard headcode box. At the same time the central lamp bracket, marker light and headboard clips were removed and longer horizontal grab rails fitted. (www.rail-online.co.uk)

A very rare pairing of two D800s on a freight duty recorded on 22 May 1966 at Tiverton Junction. At the front is D804 AVENGER which is best known for its high-speed exploits on the inaugural up run of the accelerated 'Bristolian' in June 1959. It leads D807 CARADOC which has lost one of the screwed traps below the cab floor. (www.rail-online.co.uk)

Two of the three men in the cab are eyeing up the talent while the driver enjoys a mug of tea as D806 CAMBRIAN passes a well-populated beach at Dawlish on 24 July 1961 train. The C68 headcode indicating that this is the 7.30am Padddington- Kingswear service has been chalked onto the nose end. D806 received yellow warning panels the following March during a Light Casual overhaul. (H D Ramsey)

D806 CAMBRIAN catches the evening sun at Westbury on 23 May 1969 whilst on a train of Mermaid ballast wagons. The maroon livery received in June 1966 was despite the condition pictured, to last for another eighteen months until its final Intermediate overhaul completed in March 1971; the full yellow ends were added in January 1968. (www.rail-online.co.uk)

D808 CENTAUR draws into Weston-super-Mare with the 10.45am ex Paddington in late-1961. It gained the OHLW flashes at the end of September and yellow warning panels in March 1962, and was one of only two Warships to carry green livery with full yellow ends, albeit for only around six months in early 1968, before being repainted in blue in July of that year. (Paul Chancellor)

A busy scene at Tiverton Junction on the 7 July 1971. Maroon and work stained D809 CHAMPION heads north on the 1M49 14.15 Newton Abbot-Sutton Coldfield Motorail passing D6326 with the Hemyock Milk. In the car park near the signalbox is a vintage Morris Minor police panda car parked next to what could be an early ancestor of today's 4x4s. CHAMPION received maroon livery with full yellow ends in March 1968 and was withdrawn on 3 October 1971 when the class was taken off the Waterloo-Exeter services. (www.rail-online.co.uk)

D810 COCKADE runs into Camborne on 24 August 1963. It gained the yellow warning panel in September the previous year and ran in this condition until June 1965 when it went into Swindon and was fitted with a standard route indicator panel. It wore green with full yellow ends for over two years before being repainted in the final version of blue in April 1970. (www.rail-online.co.uk)

810 COCKADE on 30 September 1972 at Basingstoke heading the Merstham-Westbury stone empties returning to the West Country. Three other members of the class (814, 825 and 829) which had previously been withdrawn at the end of 1971 were reinstated in March 1972 because of the increase in this stone traffic. COCKADE never carried maroon livery, receiving blue with full yellow ends, a single insignia and sans serif numbers in April 1970. It was one of the last three of the class in service, being withdrawn from Laira on 4 December 1972. (www.rail-online.co.uk)

Chocol
vehicle
(Hugh

D820 GRENVILLE at its birthplace after it acquired yellow warning panels in January 1962. It remained in green until May 1967 when it went into works for a Classified repair, emerging in blue with full yellow ends. It was one of the last to remain in service, not being withdrawn until November 1972. (Terry Berry)

D81
00.0
Swi
foll

An early evening scene on the Cornish main line as D823 HERMES runs through Camborne on 24 August 1963. It is hauling the 6.0pm Penzance - Kensington Olympia 'Milk', which is lightly loaded with only six 6-wheel tanks followed by a Hawksworth full brake. HERMES appeared in the full spectrum of liveries, carrying maroon with both small panel from May 1966, and with full yellow ends added by May 1968, before receiving the final version of blue in September 1969. (www.rail-online.co.uk)

D823 HERMES passing through Eastleigh on 7 March 1967 with an up freight. The maroon livery already looks well worn although it was less than a year old, and was to have full yellow ends added by May 1968 before blue was applied in late 1969.(www.rail-online.co.uk)

The green paintwork of D825 INTREPID was in a dreadful state when pictured at Bristol in July 1968 backing on to the down 'Devonian' which ran from Bradford to Kingswear. INTREPID went into Swindon in September that year for an Intermediate overhaul emerging in November wearing blue with full yellow ends. Note the multiple working equipment recently re-fitted for the 1968 double-headed accelerated West of England trains. (www.rail-online.co.uk)

D826 JUPITER at Exeter on 16 May 1971 showing why it needed to be repainted at Laira the following month. Was it the wearing qualities of rail blue or the effects of too many trips through the chemicals in the automatic washing plants? D815 DRUID keeps it company in more ways than one: it retained what is already a deteriorating maroon livery until it was withdrawn three months after this photograph was taken.

828 MAGNIFICENT at Exeter St.Davids on 5 June 1971 with the 07.15 Penzance-Paddington. MAGNIFICENT caught fire on the 1st of the following month at Nailsea and Backwell while working the 6B28 23.35 Avonmouth-Plymouth Friary freight and was withdrawn by the end of August. It had been painted maroon in early-1966 and stayed in that livery until July 1969. (www.rail-online.co.uk)

D829 MAGPIE being given a final spit and polish where it was on display at the Locomotive Engineers Exhibition at Marylebone on 12 May 1961. The exhibition was opened by the Duke of Edinburgh and in return he was allowed to drive MAGPIE to Windsor via the Wembley Stadium loop and onto the WR at Acton. D829 was chosen because the Duke had commanded the ship HMS MAGPIE from September 1950 to 1952. (Paul Chancellor)

At the start of the second week of Warship working over the ex-LSWR route D831 MONARCH stops at Axminster on 28 August 1964. The WR introduced a regular interval pattern of semi-fasts between Waterloo and Exeter to replace the express service hauled by the Bulleid Pacifics. The D800s had a virtual monopoly of the Exeter-Waterloo trains in order to simplify maintenance procedures and crew-training. (www.rail-online.co.uk)

D831 MONARCH pictured during July 1968 while shunting at Long Rock depot Penzance. On 30 November 1966 it had been the second of the class to emerge from Swindon in the new Rail Blue livery. Unlike the first D864 ZAMBESI which had the prescribed full yellow ends, MONARCH had for some reason reverted back to small yellow warning panels. It eventually received the standard Corporate Blue in March 1969.

D835 PEGASUS inside Swindon works on 24 March 1968 where it was nearing the end of a Classified repair which started on 15 February. It had been damaged in a collision which required extensive bodywork repairs, and obviously received a full repaint, with the blue livery replacing the green which it had worn since it entered service in August 1960. It was s the last Class 43 to receive an Intermediate overhaul, completed in April 1971 only to be withdrawn six months later. (www.rail-online.co.uk)

In the early 1960s the NBL Warships worked turn and turn about with their Swindon-built classmates. At Wellington (Somerset) on 14 July 1964 D836 POWERFUL roars through with the twelve coaches of the 10.45am Penzance-Sheffield, the 'Cornishman'. (www.rail-online.co.uk)

D837 RAMILLIES on 15 March 1970 at Old Oak with D848 SULTAN and Type 2 D6332. Its air intake to the right of the headcode box has been blanked off and D837 has only one of its headboard clips. It was to remain in service until withdrawn at Newton Abbot in May 1971. (www.rail-online.co.uk)

The NBL Warships were prone to oil leaks and the bodywork of D838 RAPID pictured at Old Oak Common in late June 1969 has plenty of evidence of that. Its cab and nose ends are almost as clean as when it was given a full repaint in August 1968, some two years after Swindon began repainting locomotives in blue. It was one of three Class 43s to be withdrawn without carrying blue livery. (www.rail-online.co.uk)

With its nameplates long removed, D840 had been withdrawn six months earlier when pictured at Old Oak Common on 2 November 1969. Unlike several of its classmates RESISTANCE was not given a reprieve after it was stored at Old Oak in early 1969. It lingered there until April 1970 when it finally went to Swindon for cutting-up. (www.rail-online.co.uk)

In Spring 1968 the Class 43s were moved from their unsuccessful spell on West Midlands services and took over the Worcester and Hereford trains. D841 ROEBUCK is on shed at Worcester on 7 April 1969. It has round holes cut in the headcode boxes, which were an Old Oak modification to improve the cab ventilation. It is in the early standard blue with D-prefix serif numbers and cab-mounted double arrows which it received in September 1967. (www.rail-online.co.uk)

D842 ROYAL OAK passes through Reading West during 1962 on the down Torbay Express, the 12.30pm Paddington-Kingswear. The interesting point about this picture is the white diamonds on the buffer beam, something which D842 shared with D834, a short lived embellishment which came back with a vengeance in 1968 when multiple working equipment was re-fitted to many of the Swindon-built Warships. (www.rail-online.co.uk)

D843 SHARPSHOOTER on 22 July 1967 near Torquay working the 1A39 09.55 Paignton-Paddington. It was one of those never to wear maroon livery, going straight into blue with full yellow ends in February 1968. SHARPSHOOTER lasted until 22 May 1971 when it was withdrawn from Newton Abbot. (www.rail-online.co.uk)

D844 SPARTAN runs into Taunton on 14 July 1964 with the 09.10 Kingswear-Bradford 'Devonian'. The Warships were used on these inter-regional trains to the Eastern and North Eastern Regions for many years, working as far as Bristol where they handed over to Peaks or Brush Type 4s for the journey north. (www.rail-online.co.uk)

D846 STEADFAST in pieces at Swindon Works on 14 September 1969. This variant of the early blue livery with a small double arrow above the nameplate, which it had from April 1967, was carried by only two other Warships, D830 and D847. It would be repainted in the standard final blue livery during an Intermediate overhaul between May and August 1970 and was withdrawn in May 1971. The nose end detail is distinctive – the upper lamp bracket and headboard brackets disappeared when the nose end was repaired in 1966 after it was badly damaged in a collision. (www.rail-online.co.uk)

D849 SUPERB lives up to its name when pictured at Teignmouth on 22 July 1967 with the 09.35 Kingswear-Bradford 'Devonian'. SUPERB had been released from Swindon in blue on 5 July after a Classified overhaul during which it had one engine changed and the other repaired, both bogies changed and its bodywork repaired. (www.rail-online.co.uk)

D850 SWIFT arrives at Bristol in 1967 with the 09.50 Exmouth-Manchester, a summer Saturdays Only train. It remained in green until mid-1968 and therefore went straight into blue when repainted. SWIFT spent several months stored out of traffic at Old Oak Common in 1969 but was reinstated for a further two years in service before withdrawal in May 1971. (www.rail-online.co.uk)

D850 SWIFT on a dreary grey day at Oxford on 14 September 1969. It was allocated to Old Oak Common for three years and has the additional ventilation holes in the front doors and after spending two months stored out of traffic there earlier in 1969 it was chosen for a return to traffic in May. SWIFT went straight from green into the early blue livery in May 1968, which it retained until withdrawn three years later. (www.rail-online.co.uk)

The Class 43s transferred to Old Oak Common in late-1967 for West Midlands duties were often found at Banbury on freight workings which they had taken over from English Electric Type4s. D851 TEMERAIRE is pictured there in 1968 not long after being repainted in blue at Swindon in May of that year. It worked until May 1971 when it was stored at Newton Abbot and withdrawn before the end of that month. (www.rail-online.co.uk)

D852 TENACIOUS retained its green livery until late-1969 but it was already in poor condition when pictured at Banbury in 1968. It was the only Warship to have the 'D' prefix removed while still in green, and because of the late date went straight into the final style of blue when it was finally repainted in November 1969. It has a cast-iron 81A Old Oak Common shedplate in the "Swindon position" on the front skirt and the usual additional ventilation holes applied by Old Oak common to improve the cab ventilation. (www.rail-online.co.uk)

A battered D853 THRUSTER is the worse for wear as it waits at Exeter St.David's on 27 July 1964 with the 8.20am Manchester-Penzance. One of the headcode boxes has been smashed as has a bodyside window and the paint has been damaged. The subsequent repaint including the addition of a yellow warning panel ensured that it went straight into blue livery the next time it was repainted, in August 1967. (ExeRail)

D853 THRUSTER in storage on 2 November 1969 at Old Oak Common. It had been taken out of service in early July but went to Swindon for refurbishment in March 1970. Its nameplate is red despite all blue liveried locomotives having the backgrounds painted black. D840 had been withdrawn six months earlier but, unlike several of its classmates, RESISTANCE was not given a reprieve after it was stored at Old Oak in early 1969. (www.rail-online.co.uk)

A well-worn D854 TIGER at Reading on 10 September 1968 having brought in an inter-regional freight to Scours Lane. It stayed in green following an extended works visit for collision damage repairs in mid-1967 before a repaint into blue in late-1969. (www.rail-online.co.uk)

Under the LMR wires at Hampton in Arden near Birmingham on 1 August 1968 D855 TRIUMPH with a northbound freight from Banbury and Leamington which would have joined the LM line at Coventry. Twenty-one NBL-built Warships had been transferred to Old Oak Common for West Midlands work in the second half of 1967 but after numerous failures they were taken off the London-Birmingham passenger services and confined to freight and parcels duties. (Michael Mensing)

D855 TRIUMPH heads the 6B40 11.40 Acton-Stoke Gifford through Pangbourne in either 1967 or 68. It was painted maroon in May 1966 during an Intermediate repair, a livery that would last for over three years. It spent two years at Old Oak Common in 1968/9 and has the trademark ventilation holes as a souvenir of that time. D855 was stored at Old Oak Common for much of 1969 but was called to Works in October and emerged in blue on the first day of 1970. (www.rail-online.co.uk)

D857 at Plymouth in 1963 after arrival with the 7.43am Nottingham-Plymouth on a summer Saturday. It gleams in the sunshine compared to the dull appearance of one of the early NBL D63xx Type 2s alongside. This picture shows the slightly orange-red colour of the bufferbeam which matched the nameplates on the Warships as built; this was changed to the standard pillar box red when the locomotives were repainted. UNDAUNTED was one of the first two Warships into maroon, in September 1965. (www.rail-online.co.uk)

858 VALOROUS passing the NCL Parcels Depot at Gloucester Central on 16 June 1971 with the 5B73 10.30 Bristol Malago-Worcester Vans. Its next diagrammed working would be the 1A26 14.15 Worcester-Paddington. Like many of its surviving classmates it was withdrawn at the start of the Winter timetable on 3 October 1971. (www.rail-online.co.uk)

D859 VANQUISHER at an Old Oak Common Open Day on 15 July 1967 - in the recently acquired early incarnation of Rail Blue with serif numbers and two sets of double arrows. For some reason which remains lost in the mists of time, VANQUISHER was the only Warship to have long side grab rails on the nose end. (www.rail-online.co.uk)

The North British-built Warships were rarely seen at the London end of the Southern Region. D860 VICTORIOUS was captured heading a Special Stock Working through Clapham Junction on 27 June 1967. Its green livery was to last until 1968 when it was repainted in blue with full yellow ends. (www.rail-online.co.uk)

D861 VIGILANT on a Class 8 freight at Tiverton Junction in August 1970. It had been allocated to Newton Abbot since June 1965 and spent the rest of its days there, apart from a few weeks at Old Oak Common in mid-1969. It gained the maroon livery in September 1966 and was the last maroon Warship with a small yellow panel, which it kept until its final Intermediate overhaul in early 1971. (www.rail-online.co.uk)

862 VIKING at Plymouth Laira soon after it finally received new paintwork in April 1970 having been in store from the start of that year and returning to traffic after an Intermediate overhaul. Its reprieve was relatively short-lived and it was withdrawn in October 1971. (www.rail-online.co.uk)

D863 WARRIOR on shed at Bristol Bath Road on 12 July 1964. The photograph clearly shows the characteristic NBL roof detail of diagonally opposed exhaust ports and raised radiator fan housings. The five pairs of ventilator flaps are still open – these were manually operated and often seized in this position. WARRIOR was an early casualty of the BR Traction Plan, being withdrawn in March 1969. (www.rail-online.co.uk)

D864 ZAMBESI, the first Warship into blue livery in November 1966, had dark brown bogies and underframe, following the BR Design Panel's first painting instructions to the letter. It is shown here in May 1967 a few days after emerging from Swindon after collision damage repairs. Its numbers were originally placed under the engine room windows and the BR double arrows under the cabs, but when ZAMBESI was repaired these were moved to the then standard positions, although it retained the dark brown valance which it kept until withdrawal. (Modern Image Slides)

D865 ZEALOUS at Bradford on Avon in June 1968 with evidence of the floods which hit the south west that summer. When it was delivered from Glasgow in June 1962 it was the last Warship into service. It lasted until May 1971, by which time it had been repainted into blue livery, in August 1969.

In the second week of July 1968 D866 ZEBRA and D823 HERMES prepare to depart from Penzance on the 10.15 'Cornish Riviera Express' to Paddington. The mix of tatty green and maroon liveries is somewhat short of the BR Corporate image for the Western Region's prestige train! ZEBRA went into Swindon later in the month for an intermediate overhaul, emerging in blue with full yellow ends. HERMES, maroon since May 1966, had only acquired the full yellow ends a couple of months earlier and did not go into blue until September 1969.

D867 ZENITH received yellow warning panels in August 1962 and is seen at Swindon with its bufferbeam repainted in that rather peculiar orange-red colour; although the green on the nose has been repainted the body side paintwork has not been re-touched. The red-backed 83D shedplate was used for Plymouth Laira until September 1963 when it became 84A. (Terry Berry)

On 7 May 1969 a maroon-liveried pairing of D867 ZENITH and D870 ZULU arrive at Exeter from the ex-LSWR line with the diverted 10.30 Paddington-Penzance. ZENITH was repainted maroon in late-1966 and eventually received blue in September 1970. ZULU went into maroon in late-1965 and had full yellow ends applied in May 1968. (Railphotoprints)